T0167204

THE
JOURNEY
OF LIFE

I Live and I Learn . . .

KELE SENKHANE

Order this book online at www.trafford.com
or email orders@trafford.com

Most Trafford titles are also available at major online book retailers.

Printed in the United States of America.

ISBN: 978-1-4669-4953-9 (sc)
ISBN: 978-1-4669-4952-2 (e)

Trafford rev. 11/06/2012

 www.trafford.com

North America & international
toll-free: 1 888 232 4444 (USA & Canada)
phone: 250 383 6864 ♦ fax: 812 355 4082

ACKNOWLEDGMENTS

I would like to thank the Most High for bringing persecution and trouble in my life. I am immensely grateful for them more than I would be grateful for answering my prayers. If it was not for that, I would still continue being lifeless. Now I know before I perform any other worldly purposes, the main purpose I have is to serve, praise and give honor to God Almighty all the time. I am truly thankful for the cup of persecution given. It was bitter and hard to swallow, but very sobering.

DO WE GET TO ACHIEVE CONTENTMENT?

What is it that ever provides absolute contentment? Social believes proclaims financial acquisition and freedom brings contentment. I frequently quest for it from diverse sources of life, merely to discover a brutal and unbearable truth. It is something that is abstract and priceless. I believe I possess and regularly acquaint myself with financial, moral and spiritual consciousness. I also get to discover personal standards and values are often being strayed and compromised to acquire financial freedom.

Affection and admiration towards possession for optimum materialistic tangibles, is what I have. Due to human nature, I admire to have the luxurious car, town house on the hill with glass wall and elevator inside (I know, you probably saying to yourself, elevator in your glass house?;) However, we all want the same things, we want to be loved and we aspire to attain the best in our lives. I admire to have clothes of the highest quality, design, trend and class. I admire to have a partner whom I will share my dreams and desires with. A partner that aids and offer support in everything I engage in. I admire to have a family one day. I admire to be successful in all my involvements and life endeavors. I fundamentally wish to make it and working towards attaining established objectives and to be successful.

Life on the other hand, does not entirely correspond to plans and anticipated outcomes as we think. Life has no guarantees. Life is simple. According to my experiences, life contains one certainty that is uncertainty. It is perplex at times to uncover a vivid and comprehended meaning of what life is. Perception and philosophy towards the meaning of life varies from each and every one of us. The truthful knowledge and understanding of life is known by the Supreme Being. Life is an absolute repetition. Whatever phenomenon that is current, it's definitely not extraordinary or foreign. Life is learning from encountered experiences. Life has unexplainable fluctuations. I personally reckon life is just to be. In life if you are driven by money to be content, then you are chasing the wind.

I spend time of my life laboring, working and what do I have to show for it? Generations come and go but the world does not change. What happened before will happen again. I discovered that even if I owned more riches than anyone else, I realized it would not mean anything. People work hard to succeed because of the envy of others. It is useless because even if you achieve, you still won't be content. It's better to have only a little with a piece of mind, than to spend time chasing wind.

Growing up I have come to realize people always posses a Perception the grass is always greener on the other side. When you on the outside and looking in, everything looks attractive, *however when you step closer, the picture has a complete astray sight to what you have imagined. Elaborating further on the above mentioned phrase, you would think we are absolutely content with ourselves, with what we have, with where we are, with who we are, merely to uncover entirely the opposite, we are faced by misery. After my High School period, I decided to be an academic and empower myself with academic knowledge, however the rationale behind this resolution was to have the means to pursue material success as our generation is constantly exposed to society pressures and expectations where accomplishments are entirely scaled by the kind of car, residence or clothing one acquires.*

The lack of elements that defines and flags out "what success Is!" in our daily lives usually connotes and implies failure; you also need to keep in mind that people have varied definition of success. In our days, most of the times, not to be perceived as a failure, normally people tend to be subjected to society pressures and engage in activities forcing them to meet demands of society. It is interesting how distance creates an illusion. An illusion in a later stage gives true reality once you approach events of life with profound and mature perception. It comes with believe that everyday we are being misguided. Once there is lack of a firm and proper foundation of guidance from the beginning of our actions and in whatever we do, we will remain miserable.

People spend their entire life for financial pursuits and life is completely natural. Money is vastly necessary ! Money unlocks abundance of alternatives and gives liberty from poverty. Money is resourceful but also equivalently dangerous.

We get to witness people who are rich and reckon money brings ultimate joy. Permit yourselves to take time and perceive them, you will get to encounter an unexpected outcome. That the more money one acquires the less peace acquired. The world we live in contributed and managed to corrupt our thinking process. There are human tendencies of competing with one another, in the latter we fail to realize competition should be with ourselves. We need to live our own lives, be authentic and not be a duplicate of the next person.

I came to realize, an individual who engages in this kind of competiveness, brings challenges to themselves and does not realize losing yourself yields into discontentment in the end. I find that it is crucial to learn; to grow our perceptions of what the true meaning of contentment is. As communities and eventually the world, we need to change how we view material acquisition as a means to fulfilling ourselves, I get to understand that no worldly measures brings internal joy. We establish objectives, we have dreams and desires, we would like to attain one day, and we frequently search for what will make us content and hope to discover that through achieving our goals and dreams.

This is what occurs in majority of minds. You long for something to happen, but when it does occur you get to see you are still discontent. That what you longed for, does not bring you the joy you had hoped for and in turn something else begins to create a misery within you. It is something that needs to be understood, if your desire is not fulfilled, you get frustrated and if your desire is fulfilled, then too you are not fulfilled because it would not make you happy as you hoped. It is sad to undergo such and in most cases I realize that we confuse reasons of motivation. For example, where one does what they love due to their passion and love what they do, there are motivated, but when person works simply for a pay check reasons, they are not motivated, but rather moved. They are moved to work in order to get paid, nothing else! To be content is to decide to be happy with what you already have. How to be content is something we all have to learn. You can have the joy in every single day by being satisfied with what you have and what you do. You do not need to want what others have or desire to do what they are doing. Always remember that to have someone else's life you get to the good parts of their life, but going to experience the bad parts as well.

Not to be misunderstood! Money can be viewed as a motivation. Money can bring you happiness. Money can also serve as motivator if the reason is to satisfy needs and wants. For example, benefits that are received in companies, do not motivate, but rather moves potential and capacity to a standard degree. To be a motivated person, one needs to perform constantly above the normal degree, accelerate your competence level further and further until you reach the your goal and also get to see how far you can go. Maturity, opportunities, accountability and passion builds a strong and assertive foundation of motivation. And Yes! Money drives and motivates one to achieve. Just as when companies gives employees raise or fringe benefits and everyone is happy for a while. However, in a long run, the discontent reemerges. Our minds are cunning. The mind wants to enter into the world not for you to ripe, but because of all the oppressed feelings that are constantly seeking their fulfillment. The mind will never permit you to be content. Regardless of conditions you find yourself in. The mind will always look for something to be discontent about. A mind is tool that creates discontentment?

Give yourself a challenge. Should you let go of your mind, suddenly you will get to find that you become content for no reason at all. It will then indicate that contentment is natural, it is to be at your natural self, similarly to when you inhale and exhale. Its something that you are unaware of, you simply go on breathing without thinking. Being content is not an outside condition, it is simply there and that is being you. Bliss is a natural state; it is not an objective or something you achieve. Once you step out of your mind, you will begin to feel contentment. I take a look at mad people at times some are content and happy more than the so called sane people. Please, do not get me wrong. I am not saying be mad but rather be mystical. Mystics is the most peaceful and harmonious synthesis. They have that entire reasonable person. They are whole; they are complete.

The life is here and the life is now. If your basis of contentment is weighted by worldly acquisition, that means your happiness has been conditioned and means you will remain unsatisfied. If you fail to be content currently in spite of it all, you are never going be content. The mind keeps telling you, have this, have that. Be this, do that . . . Otherwise you not go to be happy. You have Big Car, Big house, now you need to own a mountain, then you going to be satisfied.

Unless you are simply content for no reason at all times, you going to struggle to be content. You will always find something *destroying your happiness and tranquility. You will always find something missing. And you never achieve a state where everything is available. Even if it were possible, then too, you would not be content.*

We go on procrastinating what is meaningful. All that rotates in our mind is money that has to be gathered . . . more power, more money, more cars and islands. In a mist of such pursuits, we subside to chase spiritual nutrition. Once you have accumulated, you get to find yourself slowly drowning in a sea of discontent. Then what? It's crucial to pursue your dream and objective for the right reasons (With that said, keep in mind the rationale of personal pursuits varies from each individual.) Society needs to change a generic manner of looking at things. Take time to regularly pay attention to the mechanism of the mind, if everything was readily and easily available, we would suddenly feel bored and lonelier than before.

THE GREED MONSTER

G reed is a serious challenge that our communities, countries and the world as whole are facing, it is a challenge that desperately needs rapid attendance. Selfishness is a problem frequently faced in parliaments, workplaces, countries, churches, our homes and communities. People think of themselves first and will do anything at any costs, to get ahead.

Greed may be defined as an act of stuffing yourself with something and have too much of it, no matter the sufficiency limits. Being greedy often indicates a fear of an internal or external void. Normally when we are timid to be empty, either for internal or external reasons, we want to somehow acquire more and more things. It is just never enough, a person wants to go on overindulging themselves unnecessarily to conceal or eliminate the void experienced. Society often perpetuates the idea that being empty means the end of the world, which is not it at all! There is vast contribution and investment by society to this concept, we not aware is being fed to us. This is a concept that drives people to be greedy, people to be driven by money and power. A concepts that creates a whole structure of power *and money orientated community, a society merely driven by material and will not stop at nothing to acquire them.*

Just as anyone who is victim of public attention. They want everybody to be at their disposal. They are constantly seeking for attention and to look up to them. I guess it's a human nature to be fond of high preference and consideration. Attention is a drug and many are enslaved by it. Imagine you passing through your own town and no one pay any attention to you, not getting any recognition, not getting any attention at all. Or you get passed and not being noticed. How will that make you feel? I am most certain that majority of people are not going to like not being noticed. Every one seeks a degree of acknowledgement. If it is not received, you feel like you are a nonentity, a no one. It will be like you have been reduced to nothing.

People are frequently on a quest for more and more attention. Some people look for attention through fame, well recognized celebrities engage in publicity acts to stir attention or ordinary people quest for it through criminal activities, just to get noticed. Being a saint and being in your little corner does not get you recognized, therefore rather be a murder, be involved in what creates a stir to be reckoned. Which is absolutely absurd?

As humans, we are slaves of our own desires. We are caged by our desires and have remained to be victims of unnecessary material acquisition. Anyone with power utilizes their power to get what they want. The more we have and get, the more we want and in some cases, depending on various circumstances, the behavior of being greedy progresses. We then escalate at being greedy people.

Everyday of our lives, we witness how leaders abuse their powers and capacities. Where there is power held by a greedy leader it is more detrimental than the worst dictator. Dictorship its good when used and implemented accordingly and properly. It is vital and there is a desperate need to be cautious of the people we choose as leaders and ambassadors. The decisions we take should be our accountability as a nation. It is of high significance to model acts of solidarity. The world deteriorates due to greed and selfishness; we have selfish leaders in parliaments, governing countries. This structures and models an incorrect behavioral practice among communities, countries and gradually to the entire world.

Just imagine a world where people are not greedy. Where you get to have the rich and middle class understanding that no one in world deserve to starve, to lack clothes and a shelter. Extending a hand and offer help were necessary with the aim to descend poverty in the world. If the world was of people that are not greedy, we would have an entirely different world, a more beautiful place to live in. Violence and poverty would be challenge we hardly faced with. There would be less of accumulating to fulfill personal interest and certainly be more love, more peace, more joy, more dance and music. People will not only have the gadgets in their big houses, but they will be more alive.

If the world was not greedy, people would begin to be more fulfilling to their needs. Needs that are not desires. Desires are unnecessary, needs are necessary. And desires are endless. Desires continuously go on to ask for more, but needs are simple and can be fulfilled. Greed is spiritual problem. People are taught that if you do not have many things, you are nobody. Therefore, people go on overindulging. It does give temporary relief but sooner or later you begin to feel empty again.

A VICTIM OF SELF DOUBT

S elf doubt! That sounds familiar. I have been a victim of self doubt on many occasions. I grew up in a very stable, disciplined and strict household structure of two bothers and both my parents. I highly take pride in my family and how I was and still being raised, although at times I feel that, the upbringing system implemented and utilized was stretched a little bit too far and unnecessarily exercised.

As I my years ascended and got older, realization hit me that the upbringing approach I got exposed to, I was loved and cared for. My parents just wanted to yield a responsible, assertive and disciplined grown up. To achieve that, they were very strict in their upbringing and I believe that it prohibited adequate liberty and sphere to express my thoughts, fears, and emotions without to being viewed as being rebellious and disobedient to them. My communication got more and more paralyzed, I became confidence deficient, in my own opinions and having discussions regarding anything. Therefore, Although I had concerns that I was not happy about, to challenge them was a problem as I was always timid of being unnecessarily reprimanded. I opt to be less vocal and expressive of what

I thought and believe in. I used the non vocal behavior or character to escape the occurrence.

I reckon growing up in this kind of family structure made it acceptable to proceed with a self doubting behavior. It's interesting how one becomes unconsciously habituated to a behavior? It became normal not have an opinion, not to voice authentic feelings. But I slowly learned to surrender from the behavior, and developed a vocal attitude. When I am solitary and thinking of my dreams and objectives, there inner voice would whisper and reassure me that I have all the potential and competence to achieve my dreams and objectives. But it would be a different ball game when I am in the real world, where I have to prove to myself and the world of what I am capable of. I deeply know that I can do it, but somehow the doubt would creep up on me and distract what motivates and keeps me focused. I have learned that in order to accomplish anything I needed to face my fears. I had to find ways to refrain from doubting myself. I took time to reflect on my weakness, strengths, values and objectives. Remind myself at all times that I am here in this world for a reason and for a meaningful purpose. I possess a unique and substantial existence and that's more than reason enough to prosper in my endeavors.

Do you ever have that feeling after a bright idea hits you and just before you realize what is wrong with it? You postpone that sudden departure of excitement by evaluating it. I have had that on many occasions. It's important to give an idea or yourself time to grow and breathe so that the excitement of an idea proceeds. It may reveal new possibilities. Take guards of self critics and doubt away from your mind. We tend to criticize ourselves and our ideas far too soon. Criticism especially the whole negative kind can be like a cold, white frost in spring. It kills off seeds and budding leaves. If we can relax our self critical and skeptical guards then we shall be more productive performers. Do not let evaluation interfere with mind fluency.

We need to avoid spiraling into the cycle of self doubt; I believe that it's useful to reflect on why we feel compelled to make these assumptions in the first place. We live in a culture that is so busy and fast paced that we do not stop and take time to look deeply within, both at ourselves and around us. We tend to think that we are the only one with hang ups because society is not truthful about feelings and insecurities. For instances, if someone asks you how you are, it's likely that you response would be: "Great, thanks!" when really deep down you are depressed and anxious. It is not uncommon for people to have feelings of doubts even for those who are at top of their fields do suffer from feelings of self doubt and inadequacy. The outside world would never reckon that these people suffer from these issues, but they do because they are human.

Opinions are the cheapest commodity on earth. Everyone has flock of them and ready to be wished upon anyone who will accept them. If you are influenced by opinions when making decisions, you will not succeed in any of your planned undertakings. Take no one into your confidence except the capacity of you mind. Majority of people carry inferiority difficulties with them through the rest of their lives because some well-meaning but ignorant person destroyed their confidence through opinions.

I have had an encounter in my path, that there are people who have a veneer of knowledge. Such people generally talk a too much and do less listening. There is also a particular projection of confidence. When you are talkative people perceive you as a confident person and if you talk less you are perceived to have a low self esteem. Keep your eyes and ears wide open and your mouth closed if you envy to have a habit of prompt decision. Experience has taught me that those who talk much do little else. If you talk more than you listen, you prevent yourself of many opportunities to acquire resourceful knowledge. You also reveal your plans and purposes to those who take great delight in defeating you because they envy you.

Any sensible person should be open to critics; however there is time and place for everything. There are unnecessary critics that are thrown to destruct rather to construct and develop a person, to merely inflict self doubt and undermine their capacities. This is why I learn to rarely talk about work in progress, unless it is of course necessary.

☞ MY PURPOSE!

I have always asked myself and currently posing this question. What is my purpose? What is the reason of my presence? What am I here for? I tell you, I am on quest for an answer to that every day of my life. The most powerful step is to be present in the world and to be aware of your existence. As much I know how obvious that sounds, but functioning outside your purpose, it's what sets us astray from the happiness we constantly seek and desire.

After completing grade 12 I had to make a choice of professional discipline I wanted to follow. However I battled immensely to select a career path or for that matter what I wanted to do in life. At the age of eighteen I lacked a profound knowledge of who I was, what I want to be or even where I want to go. You are often uncertain of the life path you would like to take and your established five year plan seems to be too silly and too ambitious. In the mist of life path uncertainty, I chose to further my studies as an Internal Auditor. One thing I can tell you, I chose the accountancy faculty not because I was passionate and wanted to be an Auditor, but because it is a respected profession, it could get me a decent occupation and

I met the requirements needed to be an Auditor. So, I thought why not practice the profession, when I adequately meet the prerequisites? I embarked onto an accounting path, I obtained an Internal Auditing Diploma, however battled to get job as an Auditor. And decided since I was not really passionate about the field, rather endeavor to get into an entertainment as model or singer. That is where the ambiguity commenced in my life.

I was affected by quarter life crisis; I find that I am still a victim of the phenomenon. A lot is happening in terms of career path quests, relationships and family. I am constantly trying to figure out issues that concerns me and add on to the puzzle each day. Going through this life transitional period does not make it any easier to cope with challenges posed. In our modern generation we are taught to believe that you can achieve anything we put our minds to and that when it comes to things like career or travelling, the opportunities are endless. But again, reality can be quite sobering. As I grow up, I get to realize, the narrower the gap between expectations and reality becomes, and the happier and more satisfies people are. So if your expectations in life are too high, you may be setting yourself up for feelings of failure.

In addition to this, I find it difficult to settle in a career I don't truly love and enjoy. I have a feeling that I am doing what I am not supposed to do. I constantly struggle to figure out what I am truly good at between accountancy, modeling, singing and an entrepreneur. I ended up realizing that accounting is not my passion and thought modeling is. The next thing I transitioned to a modeling industry, which turned out to be not what I thought it would be, I decided to fuse that with being an artist. In all this professional path endeavors I have embarked on; I realize a lack of anticipated fruitful outcome regardless of my investments in them. At the back of my mind I know that I was made to shine, to blossom and prosper in any avenue I resolute to embark on, but still no anticipated results surfaces out of anything I do. Is due to a lack of passion, hard work, patience or focus? Or is it due to the appropriate time planned by the Most High? I am constantly posed with queries of such and battle to have an explanation. I know I have qualities needed to achieve established goals, still invest necessary qualities needed to achieve and making it. However queries remain and revisits, where am I going wrong? What am I not doing right? Why am I not getting results when I have done so much? Why I do I feel as if there is no progress in what I do.?

Another thing I have discovered is that young people are brought up to believe that if we study hard and get good grades then the world is our oyster, full of easy to find opportunities. But in reality, in the real world one struggles without any work experience, newly qualified and (often over qualified) graduates find themselves working for low paid boring jobs, struggling to pay off exorbitant student debt.

In addition to this, the current economic climate state does not make it easier for the youth. I began to experience a quarter life period, it got particularly difficult on my socially life too. It is hard not compare yourself with your friends, which in a later stage bound to make you feel inadequate. All my friends are earning vastly different salaries, some are travelling, some are getting married while others are playing the field, and some are even having children and buying their first homes. That makes one feel little left behind, although you aware that one should not unnecessarily contrast themselves to others. It happens! But then again, even if you have found a perfect job, it does not guarantee your true happiness. You may be unhappily single and jealous of friends travelling the globe even if you have perfect job!

As much I know it's important not to contrast myself with accomplishments of others and to merely focus on my path. I need to understand that as people things do not occur similarly for all of us. Others do not work hard at all to achieve or invest too much effort, but some how they still achieve. It may be due to chance or previously advantaged backgrounds. While some have to strive hard to achieve and get to yield their fruits of their labor way later. Therefore, every time I go through the self questioning and attempt to dismantle the rationale of things, I learn to comprehend what occurs in my life, I remind myself that as people we are unique and have different paths. Therefore things will not transpire according to our expectations and similar ways. LIFE IS JUST NOT THAT EASY!

To deal with the crisis, is often a huge challenge. In extreme circumstance, to be able to cope with the crisis, I would go off the deep end, by overdoing the drinking and partying. This is what most of the youngsters do to overcome the crisis. This is a mechanism used to escape their posed challenges, regardless of how self defeating it seems. It became a challenging battle of which I did not know how to overcome? I realize to further my studies, having a degree won't always provide the desired outcomes. *I also feel that the quarter life period is a better time to discover who you are. It is a time where your character and strengths are tested. They say patience is a virtue. Therefore, we need to hold on to our dreams and keep on working to achieve them. Things happen in their own time; prayers are answers when it is the right time.*

TIME TO FORGIVE
YOURSELF AND OTHERS

I'm certain that many people are guilty of not forgiving. But if you want to be free, if you want to have joy in your life, you need to learn how to forgive and forget. Why do we need to forgive? We need to forgive because we eventually torture ourselves when we don't forgive others. Bitterness and not forgiving only builds resentment within us. We need to forgive people who have hurt us. I have been hurt a lot in my life and grown to be bitter, I realized that I am only hurting myself in the end. Therefore, as people do you wrong you need to forgive them so that you can also be forgiven in return.

Now and then I tend to encounter a sad realization that you may be anguished by others for no particular reason. There are times where a person unintentionally or intentionally hurts others. In the period of my upbringing, I have encountered and learned diverse characteristics in people. I also understand you need to forgive yourselves and others to acquire optimum internal tranquility.

Every one in their personal life journeys, are at times faced and compelled to take difficult decisions in their lives. In addition to this, decisions one takes may lead as a contributing element of an anguish and hurt the other or yourself. The choice you opt to take today has the potential to build or destruct the future of your life. There are predicaments I have been part of, where I have to make solitary choice. And irrespective of advices I receive regarding a difficult situation I would be faced with. I discovered the need would arise to take an unfavorable resolution due to circumstance presented at that particular period, although I do not want to opt for it.

At times we get to make mistakes and do something detrimental to ourselves. In that, it is also crucial to surrender all your past negligence by acknowledging your inappropriate conducts to be able to heal, obtain peace and be able to move forward by learning from them. The healing process leading to self forgiveness is achievable whether you are solitary or not. You need to take time to introspect yourself and the errors committed. This would determine whether you are moving through the experience towards forgiving yourself and responding towards the situation optimistically. You need to establish the rationale for doing what you do in order to begin cleaning yourself internally.

The cleansing involves removal of some junk, clutter and trashy grudge detrimental to having inner freedom. The harbor of emotional closets is an outgrowth of your inner mind. It is important to let go of issues bothering you, caused by others and yourself as restoring the anguish gradually grows within you. And sooner or later you are unable to express what you feel; you get in mode of reacting to things in an inappropriate manner. It makes one provoked when being wronged. It is important to realize, the heart bleeds when it is hurt. We need to have willingness to move on to be free of toxic emotions. To begin to tell yourself that you are forgiven and to let others know that they are forgiven as well.

EMBRACE INDIVIDUALITY AND DIVERSITY

C hanging your destiny begins with you and being aware of your existence often pays dividends ultimately. You need to understand who you are, how you function, know your resources and how you can use them to establish the best out of your own efficiency. Most of the time, we unconsciously adopt and get influenced by opinions, behaviors, values and attitudes we get from the societies and communities that we grow up in. We need to learn to acknowledge that we are people with diverse characters, perspectives and thoughts.

It is of a common occurrence, which has grown to be socially acceptable to behave and live identically to your neighbor. Not having to follow or duplicate others ways of acting and living, means you are at liberty to live the lifestyle that you prefer and mostly comfortable with, not having to unnecessarily contrast yourself to others and not have to live up to predetermined standards. It's actually ok, to be and allow yourself just being you. I always thought everything elders did was justified. I always gathered that as child you are not allowed much of *a platform to say much as you are as child and need to seize what is being declared without questioning.*

That the only way to behave and react to situations is to follow elder's characteristics and ways of doing things all the time. Then as I grew up, being a teenager and a young adult, I gradually moved into a phase where I began practicing to be an independent thinker. That is, learning from elder's however also learning to have my opinions and perspective towards life's events.

As I gain life experience, I question all that comes my way and make decision based on my own research. I apply wisdom and lessons I receive from every influences and in someway fuse what I have experienced in making decisions. It is helpful to surround yourself with a lot of information, be curious to learn the unfamiliar to grow as this cultivates ones character. Be able to be selective from what you learn, without having to forfeit your individuality. In addition to this, we need to give ourselves a permission to be different. Take children of divorce, for instance. Statistics indicate that they are more likely to have broken marriages too. In most cases, they will believe the solution to the problems in their marriages is to end the relationship as well, because that is what their parents did. But that does not mean you need to go the same route. You are not them—you are the only one who can ask and answer this: 'how do I want my life to pan out? Yes, you may be product of your parents. They may have taught you significant lessons, but that does not mean you should act, think and behave as they did. That does not mean you should relinquish yourself in the process.

It is important to embrace diversity not only in words and actions, but in our heats as well. Let's be real. Many of us get upset when others make funny comments about our own cultures, but in private we get to laugh at others and make jokes about their cultures different to our own. We need to get the kind of negativity out of our hearts. One reason that people do not accept differences is that, they spend too much time judging each other. We waste so much time on other people. Judging their hair, the way they talk, their clothes and everything. In advance to the subject, after varsity I had to quest for employment and notice that there is lack of individual and diversity acceptance in our societies. An experience I had in corporate world, I find it important for employers to have open mind when recruiting employees. It is also crucial to understand and accept that culturally, not everyone is identical as you and just because they look different or dress differently, does not mean they are different.

It becomes intriguing how human nature wants to associate with people they are comfortable with. It is natural to feel a conjugation with someone who is from your neighborhood. People often cling to such ideologies when selecting a team they are seeking. Other than that, people need to open their spirit and learn to be more open minded and receptive. People should not have to withdraw or be reserved from being themselves because others do not understand their culture. Take a deeper look at the people's inner spirit and surrender yourselves from teasing and undermining the next cultural statements.

I find that cultural diversity in our society will help people get out of their own cage and be more open minded. When one is merely acquainted to stereotypical views culturally, then they are living in a cage . . . . . Regardless of their culture, without diversity you living in cage that needs to be unlocked to get you liberated.

But if you bring an unconcealed etiquette to look at diversity and deal with contrasts with a much more vivid perspective, you will get to see other opportunities that are out there. Endeavour to bring a diverse melody to your sphere to have a different and unusual chorus to your song; you will get to see how life becomes interesting!

EXPRESS YOURSELF
WITHOUT LIMITS

I certainly used to limit a lot when comes to expressing myself. Every time when I have to be vocal, I would think that I might be wrong and make a joke out of myself. I get to worry that my ideas would fail. This reminds me of a time when I was in primary school Grade 6. A class teacher initiated an activity where school kids were given an opportunity to cast for stage play. We were required to impersonate our favorite actors to evaluate our acting abilities. What I did was limit chances of partaking in the show by not being expressive. I chose an acting piece that was mostly favorable to me, where I had to act as being very disappointed by friend who lied to me. I tell you, I knew I had what it takes to pull it off and get into the play. I knew that I had it in me as I was always intrigued by how actors are able to modify their characters from time to time and effortlessly portray the required scripted personas with a blink of eye. The moment I casted, I got rapidly overcrowded by thoughts. Thoughts of whether I am adequately competent? I worried that people are going to find my piece as joke. That people are always ready to tease me. OMG!! They going to think I am a fluke. Instead of focusing on the play, as much as I believed in my capacity, I ended messing up, not delivering and expressing the character to the best of my ability.

To be honest, I still get to go through the same thing in adulthood; I just learn to be more aware when it emerges and to deal with it rapidly. What is different now is that I do not panic and stress as previously. In fact I choose to go astray from such reactions. I commenced with being more spiritually acquainted with the Higher Being. I discovered that it keeps me calm; it provides me with mental and emotional tranquility.

In that way I feel that I am able to cope with toxic reactions better than before. I can hear God telling and reassuring that I am deserving of this and competent. And that one day, with hard work and persistence I will get to realize my dreams. Being reassured that it does not mean it's the end when failures are encountered. It definitely does not mean it's the end of the world either. One thing I learned in my life path is a challenge of being emotionally dishonest with self. How I fail to acknowledge what I feel. I defy expressing my legit inner emotions. I have been a victim of this all my life. I can say I still am a victim. When I am sad or unhappy about something and asked how I feel about it. I rather lie than to make the other unhappy. I began to realize that we unconsciously act in this manner out of timidity or sensitivity. That somehow, what I feel are emotions that not supposed to be known, in order to safeguard others from being hurt.

Without realizing it, we do it mostly when we are ambiguous and uncertain of ourselves or our emotional journey. I always *thought to myself, that the greatest factor that averts a person from an emotional truth is our learned feedback to what we have been taught about the correct and incorrect etiquette to what we feel. In majority of our societies, It is alright to feel what makes you unhappy. You just have to keep accelerating with your life as per normal, without being vocal.*

I grow up in family that holds brief conversations about emotional expression subjects. This has yield, in return to be an introvert in character. I struggle in a major way to relinquish from this. I frequently get socially affected and not able to disclose my inner emotions eloquently and fearlessly. I get confused most of the time when it comes to an appropriate way to express what I feel. My upbringing contributed to this, as parents unconsciously taught us to conceal inappropriate response or feedback to events, and in doing that, they unconsciously taught me to suppress feelings and not say much. As a kid, I was taught everything about almost everything, but not of how I should feel. I was coached on what I am supposed to feel, and what not feel. This in a long run would cause the risk of not showing true emotions.

On series of occasions I tend to be provoked or provoke others, either intentionally or not. Most of the time, I would often be perplexed of how to respond and how to express my discomforts. There always been this strange reason when I was young (not disrespecting the elders though) they are at liberty to feel and express their emotions and youngster are not. Emotional censorship gradually gets composed and not being aware of it, future relationships are bound to be affected as well.

Due to a childhood experience, we sometimes deny when we feeling anger, anguish or any unsatisfactory emotions that we might be going through. I believe it is a perception people mostly familiar with and has grown to accept that anger should be expressed in a particular manner. And I get to be aware that there is a unique emotional response that is formed, which is meant to be applied in particular situations or events presented.

I used to work at bank and got into trouble, where a tab of an internet service was open on computer. It was being used by another colleague and just as I was about to log on to work, the internet tab was still reflecting, as a colleague never closed it. Talk about being at wrong place at the wrong time, my superior discovered the internet tab opened on PC I was using when she was performing rotational evaluations on the floor. She assumed that I was the one utilizing it. I knew I was innocent and not guilty of what she accused me of. She kept on pressing the matter that I was guilty and ready to reprimand me with a written warning. Therefore, tell me? How would you feel in an event of such? I know I am not guilty and have elaborated the account of how the event panned out, however she still pressed that I should be punished for what I have not done.

It is normal not be happy or anguished when being falsely accused. Irrespective of an account of rationale I provided regarding what had really occurred my superior still felt that I should be given a written warning. I began to be angry and emotionally unsettled. The tone on how I address the matter began to become briefly inappropriate. In a corporate world and ultimately in society as a whole, I realized it is critical to address matters appropriately, irrespective of the circumstances of the situation or the anguish you undergoing. A negative response that you convey towards the event posed may have the potential to deteriorate the situation and in the end you may be portrayed as the culprit, although you innocent.

In advance to the point I made about emotional expression versus the proposed event. I also came to realize that as much I do not want to censor myself emotionally as I used to. It is crucial to be conscious of spheres where I need to cautiously tone down the manner of how I convey emotions and thoughts, not to be at a disadvantage. It's a matter of learning and maintaining the expression equilibrium.

THE POWER OF WORDS

How many times have we set goals, visualized our desired outcome, created and repeated positive affirmations, and yet still not achieve what we had hoped for? It has happened on several occasions and it is simply a matter of words. Every sound we utter sends out an energy wave or prayer that aid in creating the world we experience. With every sentence we speak we are literally improving or destroying our health, relationships, finances, and more.

Words can make your life miserable or marvelous; it is up to what you say. Just as, what you think makes you what you are, words mold and shape your life because words are the expressions of your thoughts, ideas held in mind. When I was growing up, I have been told that negative words results in negative and unhappy experiences and positive words results in, happy and prospering experiences. Every time I am posed with a difficult situation, it's really not as easy as it sounds to declare optimistic words with hope things will get better. But I learned the importance of optimistic way of thought; it's the same as prayer. As much as we think praying is only done in churches or mosque, but every time you say something either negative or positive, in way you proclaiming a prayer unconsciously. Therefore, we need to be careful of what we say as what we say comes back to us.

You have power within you to make your life what you desire it to be. Your spoken word is not only powerful to make changes in your life; it is the power through which major changes come with spoken words. Regardless of every influence, you shape your life through your thoughts and words. You do this whether you are or not aware of it. When you know the power of words, especially your spoken words, you will put a guard at your lips and be very wise in what kind of words pass through your lips just as you will do the same with your ears, in that you will allow only which is uplifting, positive and life-enriching to enter and find lodging in your thinking process. In speaking words, you are literally moving substance, making a definite difference some where in some way. Most of all, you are making a definite, although seemingly imperceptible, difference within yourself and upon the conditions of your life.

One period in my life, I was a newly graduate and unemployed; I sought the help of a spiritual counselor. I had spent much on thinking and speaking in a negative, self demeaning way. Unhappiness compounded as I went from one negative experience to the other. The counselor helped to listen to myself; to really hear the words I utter, and to understand how through my thoughts and words, I had the power to transform my life through the words I used. As unbelieving as I was, at first I was wise enough to know that I need to be positive; I became ready to alter my way of thought about things. I was instructed to declare through the power of thoughts and words that positive changes will happen in me and in my life at all times. Most importantly through believing in what I declare.

The most powerful example I have ever heard about the use of conscious language—or actually the misuse of conscious language—was a story told directly by the woman who had the experience. This woman had developed an incurable disease of her eyes. She was rapidly going blind. Her physicians advised there was nothing they could do to help her. Being very determined and not liking what she heard, she turned to alternative therapists for a possible cure—something she never would have done had she not been in this desperate situation. A friend recommended she see someone that performed crystal healing. She thought that sounded ridiculous but decided to give it a try. During her appointment, the crystal healing therapist asked her to describe herself, her life, etc. and the therapist let her talk for about 10 minutes. Suddenly, the therapist stopped her and said "Did you know that in the last 10 minutes you said the words 'I hate to see' 15 times?" Words have tremendous power. Words give out energy and a message which creates a reaction in others. Everything you say produces an effect in the world. Whatever you say to someone else will produce some kind of an effect in that person. We are constantly creating something, either positive or negative with our words.

Speaking comes to most people as naturally as breathing. On many occasions our words are uttered without conscious thought; in fact we rarely stop and think about what we are saying. Thousands of words pour out of our mouths each day as our thoughts, opinions, judgments and beliefs are freely expressed. Often, however, we are oblivious to the positive or negative effect these words have on ourselves and the people around us. Reaction to our words often returns to us often in a multiplied form. For example if I speak words of judgment to a person they will judge me back, probably with more intensity as their judgment has the pain or anger caused by my words attached to it, words of kindness and acceptance will generate a warm and appreciative reaction in a person. That person's response to the words will be stronger because it will have the emotion created by the words attached to it. The power of words has a ripple effect in our life and those around us.

An important key to success in life is to understand the power of words. A word is a thought eternalized. Our thoughts do have a great effect on us even though they are internal. What we think affects the way we live our life, it affects our emotions, our attitudes and our behavior. A thought spoken, however, has even more power. It can never be taken back; it is out of our mouth and will have an effect. Our words have even more power than our thoughts because they not only affect ourselves, but the people and the world around us.

Successful people take control of their words, rather than letting their words control them. They are more conscious of their thoughts and words and the power they unleash. Successful people understand that they need to speak positively rather than negatively in order to see success. Successful people are characterized by the words that they speak. They know the importance of speaking words that will build self-esteem and confidence, build relationships and build possibilities. They speak words of affirmation, encouragement, love, acceptance and appreciation. To see more personal success, the words that we speak need to be in alignment with what we want to see being produced in our life—our vision and our dreams. Your words can determine your destiny. Even more importantly, your words can make a positive difference on the people you interact with every day. Before you speak ask yourself: Is what I am about to say going to uplift the hearer? Will it inspire, motivate, and create forward momentum for them? Will it dissolve fear and create safety and trust? Will I create a positive or negative ripple effect by speaking out these words? Let's be determined to unleash the power of words for positive change.

OVERCOMING CHALLENGES

I magine for a moment you are at the peak of life because you have just received some amazing news. You continue to ride the high for about 3 months till one day, one very moment; the rug gets pulled out from under you. You are sick from the news, you feel as if it's all a joke. You feel as if the last 3 months were just a dream you were living and now you feel embarrassed by sharing the news with so many around you.

Well you have two choices as I see it. You can either crawl in a hole, wish that life would just stop for a moment for you to catch your breath, feel sorry for yourself, wonder why, why you? Make excuses as to why you deserve to shut out the world, blame anyone 3 feet in front of you or you can choose to take the cards that were dealt and walk out even stronger than you were the day you found out the GREAT news.

Let's be brutally honest here, tell me what would you do? How would you overcome challenges thrown your way? Think of something that would stop you dead in your tracks and ask yourself what would you do? Most people tend to respond to the stress created by the initial impact of a crisis more than the actual situation. Their internal stress adds to the initial stress, sending them into a downward stress spiral, and they quickly lose their ability to maintain their composure and think clearly. You can prevent this scenario if you can settle yourself internally. Some crises are more difficult to step back from than others, and when the lives of our loved ones are involved, this process may require professional assistance. Whatever crisis you may be facing, remember that EVERYTHING is a matter of perspective. You can try to imagine the crisis was happening to someone else, and they were asking you for advice on how to deal with it. What would you tell them? It's amazing how we can know the right thing to say to our friends and family in times of need, but we rarely heed our own advice. So, if you change your viewpoint just a little, you can trick yourself into taking a step back and gaining a little objectivity.

I grew to understand that God never asks us to bear more than we can handle. The lessons encountered are not sent to punish or defeat me—when I find myself truly anguished by challenges, I can be sure that I am the one that needs to be reminded I have done enough. While circumstances and life will certainly require a lot from me, it is the added weight of my own self judgment. Patience with self and my life, my sense of failure or justice, my fears actually depletes my strength and overwhelms me. While there is high support for you during challenging times, not even heaven can remove strains that you actively impose on yourself. When you feel pushed to a breaking point, you are the one who must ease upon trying to hard.

Sometimes life is an uphill climb, we simply can't afford to carry the extra weight of self judgment and blame. It's *these challenging times where you need to be patient and compassionate with yourself. One needs to take deliberate measures to ensure that you give yourself rest, acknowledgement and involve yourself in activities that balance out the difficult times imposed. When you fail to do this, times that are meant to move you forward become punishing. You need to learn to honor yourself, appreciate your efforts when you challenged, it is an indispensable factor of all life lessons. It's an incredibly powerful and liberating understanding and in a time of growth and change, it's a skill we cannot afford to miss. I learned to exercise my own personal power in good and bad predicaments. As powerful and wise as I may be, I cannot, in most parts, choose my lessons. I cannot choose not to have a loss or change or agony in life. These are just realities of life and like it or not, part of how we learn and progress. More over being human, you cannot choose not to feel a certain amount of fear, anger or sorrow associated with your losses and hurts. You always have a choice how to treat yourself with love, and this choice means the difference between a mere demanding time and a truly painful experience. If you are unrelenting with yourself when circumstance seems to be unrelenting, you are doubling your burden. On the other hand, if you are patient and supportive towards yourself, you are balancing your burden.*

☞ FAILURES

The reason most of people fail to reach their destination is because they fail to distinguish between a setback and failure. I met a lot of setbacks and still come across them, but I got to learn and understand that setback is not a dead-end. I learned that setbacks are just a learning curve, a period where we get tested on how strong, assertive and willing we are to reach our destination. In fact, they speed up your journey towards success if you pay attention to them. Should there be something that does not work for you, you have not failed—but you have rather learned what not do the next time. Several times in my life I have suffered a lot of setbacks that society define and perceive as failures. Up to so far in my life, I have not made it in modeling industry, I have not made it as an Internal Auditor, I have not made it in any of the industry endeavored.

I bet plenty of people have written me of as a failure. However regardless of the circumstance I am currently faced with and of what people think. No matter how much people try to throw me off my game, I do not quit and still keep fighting to win. In challenging times, no matter how bad things may seem, I *learn to be assertive and remember that the only way I could actually fail is by quitting.*

It is important to notice that a lot of times the world does not put rocks in our way, instead we put them ourselves. I became aware of this, that every time I hold on to my mistakes, I am throwing a rock in my own bath. Allowing my mind to be filled up with fear and worry, that is just more rocks that's going to fill my way. Therefore, we need to detach ourselves from worry and let go of our mistakes, the road would clear up. With dedication, faith, compassion and hard work you can go long way.

But that does not mean you not going to face challenges. No matter how great faith is, at some point you are going to hit the wall. Whether you lead a successful life or not, it only depends on how you deal with the wall. Majority of the time, timid gets composed when faced with the wall and what do you do? We turn around instead of facing it. Hitting a wall does not make you a failure. You will only be a quitter once you turn way and go home; hitting the wall is simply a part of life. If your plan looks as if its not working out at beginning stage, do not look at it as a mistake; rather look at it as an opportunity to learn from it. Mistakes only cost you when you do not acknowledge them, but when you pay attention to your missteps, you can always learn from things people would call a mistake than you do from what people call success. I still learn to grow in how I look at failure, every time we fail we need to accept what happened, instead of being emotional about it or shifting the blame to someone else, try to analyze it and comprehend where you might have went wrong in the process.

I would also want to emphasize that even though you seem to have made it you still going to run into rocks. No matter how large my salary or checks grows, no matter how much I attain my goals, the rocks will never ever go away. They will certainly not go away the first time of my little success! Fear of failure is one of the greatest fears people have.

Fear of failure is closely related to fear of criticism and fear of rejection. Successful people overcome their fear of failure. Fear incapacitates unsuccessful people. It is critical to observe and be aware that there is no failure, there are only setbacks. Successful people look at mistakes as outcomes or results, not as failure. Unsuccessful people look at mistakes as permanent and personal. Whatever we have learned, we have to see them as a consequence of trial and error experience. People have learned only through mistakes. Most people self-limit their faculties. Most people do not achieve a fraction of what they are capable of achieving because they are afraid to try and they are afraid they will fail.

Regardless of your timid, you owe it to yourself to take action a bold, decisive action, do something scary. Fear of failure immobilizes you. To overcome this fear, you must act. When you act, act boldly. Action gives you the power to change the circumstances or the situation. You must overcome the inertia by doing something. Just think of this, what would you do if you knew you could not fail? What you could achieve? Be brave and just do it. If it doesn't work out the way you want, then look for other ways to tackle. As difficult as it is to maintain focus, I believe that I am winner, I was born to achieve. I need to keep pushing, as successful people do not give up. They keep *trying different approaches to achieving their objectives until they finally get the results they want. Unsuccessful people try one thing that doesn't work and then give up. Often people give up when they are on the threshold of succeeding.*

Trial and error are usually the prime means of solving life's problems. Yet many people are afraid to undertake the trial because they're too afraid of experiencing the error. They make the mistake of believing that all error is wrong and harmful, when most of it is both helpful and necessary. Error provides the feedback that points the way to success. Only error drives people to put together a new and better trial, leading through yet more errors and trials until they can ultimately find a viable and creative solution. To come across an obstacle is not to fail, but to take one more step on the path to a final success. Not having errors is unhelpful as you do not learn. In fact, one of the greatest misfortunes you can meet early in a project is premature—yet inevitably still partial-success. When that happens, the temptation is to fix what seemed to work so quickly, easily and look no further. Later, maybe, a competitor will come along and continue the exploration process that you aborted, driving on to find a much better solution that will quickly accelerate your partial one aside.

There is also a culture of perfection in communities and society: there is mindset that any failure is unacceptable. Only pure success will do. In order to retain your reputation as an achiever, you must reach every goal and never, ever make a mistake that you cannot hide or blame someone else. Imagine the stress and terror caused, due to such imperfection ideologies. Frequent cover up of small blemishes and the wild finger pointing as everyone tries to shift the blame for the inevitable hick ups and messes on to someone else. Lying, cheating, identity falsification and hiding problems until the crisis cannot be hidden any longer. When people fail to reach a complete answer because of the lure of some early success, many more fail because of their ego-driven commitment to what worked in the past. I often see this with personal encounters, especially those where I embarked into business and introduce ideas I had years ago and turned out to be unsuccessful. I began to be timid to re-attempt as I thought I might fail. This reminds me as well, of other people who cling to the past. People who are deeply invested in their egos and glories of the past that they prefer to set aside the opportunities for future glory rather than risk the possibility of failure. Such encounters made me realize that strength can become a weakness. Every talent contains an opposite that sometimes makes it a handicap. Successful people like to win and achieve high standards. This can make them so terrified of failure it ruins their lives. When a positive trait, like achievement, becomes too strong in someone's life, it's on the way to becoming a major handicap. But the more I thought about, it is normal to be scared: if what you are doing is at least worth it, fear of failure will always be a part of the process. It would not vanish completely, I guess to make it you need to learn to overcome your fear of failing, as it will be part of the process. Too often we stuck in fears. We allow to be enslaved by fear; you need refuse to be deterred by it.

For a long time I have always been conditioned to associate self worth to the outcomes of endeavors. Every time one of my ideas fails, it is as though I allow my self esteem to be eroded. I felt the failure deep inside of me: it's as if I am that *idea that flopped! Yes, an idea that flopped. But we should not think this way of ourselves if something you try does not work out, it does not mean you are a failure. It just means you're actively experimenting, that you're trying, and you're learning in the process. In that discipline, the definition to be a failure or success does not make sense. If people around you do not understand that, well it's probably because they are the ones who do not get an idea about experimenting, trying and learning. Do not be let down by their negativity. As long you keep your mind open to experimenting, do not bother if you keep failing! They will never loose sight of the person behind your failures. The people who really care about you will always support you through out.*

On a serious note, there are times I was and still am so timid towards failing that I would not be able to get up and try again. Therefore, it's better to try again although we get a little anxious of the end results, it is better to attempt than holding back due to your fears. So if you decide to live a life of "playing it safe", of avoiding failures altogether, you can be safe in the knowledge that you'll most likely accomplish your goal—after all, that's a dead easy target to take aim at. Just bear in mind you will never be able to get the most out of your life acting that way. Take this into consideration as well; should you eventually hit your big time of success, people will hardly remember your failures. So although you have not overcome your ego challenge, you still have chance: if you just keep trying to hit your big time moment, all you're mistakes will eventually disappear. ;)

☞ RELATIONS AND LOVE

When it comes to relationships, I have had my fair share of them. I am a passionate and love offering individual in general, either towards a friend, family or lover. In the duration of my relationship encounters, I got to be more observant and vigilant to what we think love is. Somewhere in the back of my mind I always had this picture perfect scenery of how love and relations are or rather should be. However, love, relationships and life preferences does not come in peaches and cream, they do not come in mushroom and roses as expected!

There is a funny thing about love. It often finds me in most unusual circumstances, in most obscure periods. In a very peculiar and blissful manner, I get to be introduced to love, be captured by its effects and eventually get to be transformed into a new being. The unfortunate part is that when the phenomenon takes place, we do not acknowledge the experience or let alone understand what is taking place. It is as if you are in a therapeutic process when you are exposed to the bliss that comes with love. The joy and happiness feels entirely new, as they are rarely experienced and accessed.

I got involved in relationships that were great, I got to be exposed to what it meant to be loved, adored, considered as high priority and be respected by a male counterpart. The funny thing about the experience is that, it emerges every time when I have no plans or think of being in a relationship. I tend to get guys who want more than dating; who often want to escalate the degree to a more serious relationship, where we get to be focused partners, who invest to grow in a solidarity relationship. However there are those where I have come across an enormous anguish and heartbreaks ☹ that were very challenging to cope with and overcome.

Life is all about love. Love is the only true meaning of life. Neither love nor life requires us to give up our identity, self worth, career objectives, preferred television program or our good common sense for that matter. For some reason we do not understand this. We tend to believe in the necessity of giving up certain things to gain something else; this is commonly believed when it comes to relationships. We need to understand that expressing love is the experience to get to understand who we are, what we can do, how we do things and what we believe in. You cannot get love externally if you lack love internally. You firstly need to love yourself, appreciate yourself, discover yourself and embrace who you are. In fact, love is the only thing we need. Love is where you can get peace. Love is your wealth, health and joy. Love is who we are, our identity. I used to go into a relationship looking for love, not realizing that I firstly need to bring love to the relationship to get love. I need to bring a strong sense of purpose into the relationship. I need to bring a strong sense of value, of who I am. I firstly need to be sincere and compassionate about the next person. I need to do be more trusting regardless of past experience.

I noticed that what I have achieved on my own, I must enter into a relationship willing to share what I have achieved, rather than being afraid that someone might take it and abort me. There is nothing joyful as being in relationship where both lovers share their joy, hopes, values, dreams and purposes together. That's what love is. When we bring these to a relationship, love becomes a great experience and enhances the beauty of life. If we do not have these things in place, a relationship lacks a meaningful substance. We constantly need to put effort to find and realize what true love is and what true love is not.

I enter into relationships expecting to be loved or accepted as I am. In some situations, I find that I would quest for love and acceptance so badly that I will do almost anything to get it. I break love rules; I break my personal values and break my standards. I allow people to get into my life, and be negative participants in it. I allow people to hurt me and allow people to take advantage of me. Although I have defined values and standards, it tends to be a challenge to omit such characters in my life, when captured in love mist? We act and do things for the sake of love; we often expect something in return. There never seem to be enough love to fill the void we have. Every time I feel that I do not have enough love in my heart or love received, I begin to quest for what can fill the void. I fail to realize that I need to demonstrate the love I seek. Till I became aware of this and the source of it, the void kept on growing deeper and deeper.

And every time I am exposed to this, I would do anything to escape the path. I would look for something distracting rather than to face the crisis I am undergoing. I would blindly believe anything a man declares their love for me, although they don't love me. Although I am vigilant individual generally, I get visually handicapped to be aware of whether I am truly loved or taken for a ride. Just because I want to escape the crisis I am going through, I would believe that I have discovered a resource that will free me from it. I would convince myself that this time I am in a substantial relationship and that it is going to work out. Every time I am in difficult relationship, I would rather choose to tolerate the hardships than to part ways and face the path of solitude.

I have come to see that people cannot fulfill your needs. They may like to, they may try to. They may even convince you that they can, but they cannot. There one thing they can do is make the need less urgent. We go on hoping that we can be fulfilled by people; we forget that they are also human and have the potential to hurt or disappoint us. We help one another to replace a pressing need with something else. We constantly search for love and God is love. We believe that we need the love from another person; but we need to love ourselves first and acquaint with the Godly love before we get to have the love from the next person. Having a car, a house, a family and a job is what I desire to have. Of course these things are important in achieving a certain degree of happiness and contentment. But what I really need is love within myself. I always thought objects and people bring greater love into our lives, but do they really bring same magnitude of love as I *think? Well on some level they do, but eventually you get see that they are not equivalent to what true love is.*

I always encountered a challenge of making prompt decisions in relationships. I would not know how to handle certain challenges. I would not know what to do when things are not working out they way I want them to. I would not know how to solve or to be vocal when I am hurt or unhappy. I get to realize that we tend to be afraid to be on our own. We tend to be scared to loose one, although they are hurting us. Because we believe the partner of your preference or qualities you are looking for in a person are impossible to have, so we settle; we accept the first person who comes along, only to be left devalued; ripped off; or anguished. Just because a person is delivering to your demands or urgent needs that do not mean they are what you really want. We compromise and learn to love. There are attributes that may be one's main prerequisite in partner, but find the partner lacks the personal prerequisites. We allow ourselves to be blinded by love, to be taken into a relationship that is unhealthy. We choose to believe what your partner has done to their previous partners, she/ he will not do it do you. You stay in relationship although you are miserable; you try to work things out even when your partner shows little interest to work through the difficulty.

Even though I get to be in relationship, I would find that I still do not know who I am most of the time. I keep trying to figure out how to make the next person happy and how to go about it in order for the relationship to succeed. And go through a catalogue of self-query. What went wrong in it? Will *things ever work out well for me? Will I ever get it right? Will I end with the preferred partner? How will I know this is right person for me? Is there a right person for anyone in first place? Well it's a challenging query, I just have to take the risk and hope for the best. This is mental battle that I go through all the time, regardless of the how my relationship status is or rather seems to be. :(*

THEY SAY
PROCRASTINATION
IS A THIEF

*H*ave you ever had to do something you needed to, but kept on procrastinating due to reluctance, fear or laziness? I have been and still a victim of the crisis. I have been intending to commence with my business aspirations for months and to write a book. Why am finally doing it now? Is it because I finally realized that I have no time on my side? No! I have school assignments to complete; I have to start preparing for exams coming up in end of the year. I have to work on a project that I need to submit a-sap! I am writing this book, embarking on my entrepreneurial journey to get away from all the daunting commitments and focus on what actually seize my attention and passion. I have procrastinated so many things in my life it even shocks me! I remember last year, I was supposed to write an exam and complete my degree, I was undergoing an ambiguous phase where I felt that I was not prepared to write, I felt I have profoundly invested in my academics for years and yet I have not found a well deserved employment or rather the anticipated reward in the faculty that I studied for.

Therefore, I decided not to write the exams and marginalize them to focus on what I like doing, my hobbies. We are in the New Year and still have to complete my studies that I could have easily written last year to get over and done with and do something else.

There is what we call a structured procrastination, a phenomenon I learned to pay careful attention to. It is a strategy that converts procrastinators into effective human beings, respected, admired for all that they can accomplish and the good use they make of time. All procrastinators put off things they have to do. To explain further, structured procrastination is an art of making a bad trait work for you, but this does not necessarily mean doing absolutely nothing. Most of the time, I procrastinate to do useful and attention seizing hobbies, like writing or seeking new information, reorganizing my personal items. I guess the reason why I find myself doing this is to escape from demanding commitments and do something important to me but simultaneously fun and enjoyable. However, procrastinating can set you back though if it's not well attended to. I try to minimize crucial mandates thinking that if I only have a few things to do, I will quit postponing and get them done.

I have a huge tendency of postponing. Even though it may be something that is regarded as helpful or harmful it may be very hard to find strength within not to give into the temptation of procrastinating. However, keep in mind that overcoming the temptation is possible and can be defeated. It can be easy and is highly recommended to cast out procrastination from your system if you are serious in living a successful life. There *are times where I discovered that putting off things is problem though. I would get into a dispute with my partner or any one for that matter, it would take me time to sort out the dispute or the misunderstanding posed. Instead of dealing with matter at hand immediately, I would rather escape the tension and deal with it later. Every time I go through such moments, I would often feel guilty about the things I did not get to do. I have been dismissed a lot due to this and got to have an uncooperative reputation. I have gathered that I procrastinate due to fear of facing disappointments and challenges. I postpone due a lack of proper analysis, planning, prioritizing and control of situation. It also happens when I am not certain and most importantly not realize what I am capable of or when responsibilities assigned are unclear.*

Procrastination is a behavioral problem. Most of the time, I suffer this curse without realizing it. It's the reluctance of doing what you need to do. And if the effects are neglected enough, it becomes a habit that is extremely difficult to get rid of. It becomes a very destructive and holding back habit!

So if you tend to procrastinate, you have to modify your behavior. Otherwise, you will never be successful! Accomplishments won't come to you if you keep putting off things. If you delay your work, your achievements would be delayed as well. Procrastination is a big problem. So avoid making it your problem.

I constantly missed out on good opportunities just because I fail to find the strength and motivation to do what should be done or need to be done. I got to learn how to win this is through modifying the way I think, behave and see things. Doing that requires a high amount of will power and dedication though. That is: most of the work is ultimately dependent on your efforts at the end of the day! So refrain from procrastinating or you will always fall behind.

DECLAIRE YOUR TRUE
EMOTIONS AND THOUGHTS

*S*ince I was growing up, I always had a constraint in disclosing how I feel. I still find it hard to tap into my feelings, to be vocal about things that I am not happy about. I grew up in a very assertive, comfortable, upbringing and no nonsense household. Where I would obtain not much of liberated platform to express how feel or what I thought. I still experience the same thing in adulthood, where I get anxious and have a mental battle about what I need to do or say as I would not want to go wrong or sound clueless. I often feel as if everything I do or say has to be proper and well calculated, I feel as if I am under constant moderation and that I am not supposed be wrong or even have to live up to predetermined expectations. I would rather not disclose any anguish posed or underwent for the sake of maintaining peace and to conform the unwanted or less preferred circumstances.

I have channeled myself to learn how to vocally reply to things more. Most of the time, I fear others opinion of me. I have self indulged in taking what is anguishing or whatever that does not sit well with me and not being upfront. I have grown used to and lack the guns to protest or vent my discomforts about certain issues. I am constantly shut off from my feelings, I try to cover them up and ignore them all the time. As I tend to place other's predilections before mine without realizing it, because I have somehow grown into an unconscious conformity. It is important for one to prohibit being affected by such an occurrence, as it denies your emotions, spiritual and thought liberation.

I am gradually developing the mind frame of adopting to be articulate, eloquent and vivid when it comes to saying how feel. Repelling to the unwanted without being timid to premature critics yet being sensitive towards others should there be prerequisite to do so. However, it is not that easy, particularly when it's a behavior I have grown to make part of my character. It's not advisable to emotionally block yourself, blocked emotions often accumulates within and forever waits to be unconcealed. And most of the times they get to be revealed or let out through minor incidents that eventually make one to be an unnecessarily intolerant character.

It is important to take ownership of what goes on inside of you. Be authentic about how feel and what you think at all times. If you do not do this for yourself, no one will do it for you. This will eventually give you psychological tranquility and freedom in return. There will be times when you have to be frank, call a spade a spade, and you would come across as being insensitive, but as long as the primary intention was not to be insensitive, rather to be true about your thoughts and emotions in particular.

TOLERATING AMBIGUITY
IN OUR LIVES

*W*hen one is often faced with loads of choices, does anything become more attractive? Being indecisive and uncertain are states on whole I do not enjoy. Any decision that I would take seems to be preferable to tolerate any form of indecisiveness. I wander around in a mist of doubt and uncertainty arising from obscurity and indistinctiveness. Nothing is clearly defined. It is all indeterminate. I am constantly hesitating. The ground is constantly shifting. There is no meaning that is unequivocal. In summary, I battle to endure a lack of clarity for a long period.

I have always had a plan of how my life must or would turn out from a young age. But, also forget that life has its own way of turning out. I am at an ambiguous phase, where a lot is happening, I lack comprehension and rationale to how life events unfolds, especially when I established a plan, implemented the required elements for it to be successful and in the latter I get to come across unexpected outcomes. It is important for one to be much more tolerant of ambiguity and apparent failure. People who do this are better at overcoming or successfully controlling the impulse to come up with solutions or make decisions prematurely. And also being decisive does not mean making rapid decision, but it means taking decisions at a right time. Then you will be able to explore the external space of the possibilities. That is the feasible ones and even those that may be way out or off the wall but somehow interest you.

I am often faced with uncertainties, mysteries, and doubts. They mostly surface without any profound reasons or explanation. I constantly quest for knowledge and driven by curiosity to develop myself. But again, one should also consider that to remain with half knowledge yields curiosity. When people find any sort of ambiguity, we get uncomfortable and even stressful. We jump into certainties, any sort of certainties for that matter, just to escape from the unpleasant state of not knowing. Similarly with a man who will not wait to find the right girl to marry, but marries to escape the state of being unmarried. There always seems to be an enormous barrier, a refusal to give yourself precisely what you in a quest for. You always feel as if you are in the state of a suspended animation, you are constantly wondering in the dark. All you have is unanswered questions, doubts, uncertainties and contradictions or no answers at all.

To come across regular ambiguous moments, leads to being anxious or creates fear that is overwhelming. I learn to be courageous about things, but that does not mean one would not experience these emotions, it would be totally inhuman. The habit of tolerating ambiguity helps to develop the qualities *of courage, perseverance and patience. These qualities in return will sustain you in the existence of any unavoidable uncertainty.*

I have difficulty to figure out or understand why I have not achieved thus far as I should, or why my life remains the same, year in year out. Even worse, it seems to be in reverse. I feel as if my life is going nowhere rapidly, and that my circumstances deteriorate instead of getting better. Not that I am not contributing to make my life the success that it should be, but because life has its own way of turning out. We have no control of what happens to us in life. We are faced with challenges from all walks of life, where there are happenings we have no control of, we are faced with ambiguous phases where we get to be uncertain and indecisive and would often take any decision just to flee uncertainty.

However, while we might not have any control over certain things happening, you can always have a control in how we respond to them. Your response is always your choice, and you can choose to respond in a negative or positive way. There are aspects in our lives over which you will have control, but others there is no control of them. When life happens to give us uncertainty or give us a platform to make decisions, we mostly make negative decisions, which are not of much aid to our situation. It can lead one to stop hoping, and accept that you are not worth of victory or overcoming difficulties.

If you happen to go through such, take a time to dare yourself to be better, to dream of a better you and an awesome future. We may be going through uncertain moments in our lives, but there is always light at the end of the tunnel, matter of fact, there is always light at the end of the tunnel, it is possible for life to change for the better, you just need to believe in it! We need to start paying attention to how we respond to situations, as our response to life events have a great potential to make or break us. And your life is the projection of your thoughts, so nurture your life with awesome thoughts.

BEING HARD ON MY SELF!

I sometimes tend to judge myself to harshly, where I blame
myself for things I have no control over. Every time when
plans do not go accordingly I unconsciously blame, berate and
even disparage myself, treating myself far worse than I would
ever treat other people.

I establish high standards and goals for myself and get
frustrated if I fail to meet them. I do this ample time, and the
thought of not making it immensely decomposes me. I believe
that somewhere in our life paths we will have conflicts with
people; we also go through periods where we are unnecessarily
hard on ourselves. I constantly need to be in combat with the
inner enemy, accept its there, be aware of it to know when it
emerges and deal with it. Learn how to create a higher level of
self assurance to demolish pessimistic thoughts.

What I have grown to do, is focus on the progress and not
being perfect. I always strive to be perfect in what I do, (well
not perfect, probably close to it). However I would not want to
make mistakes or be wrong. This happens because of internal
negative message we picked up from people around us. I hear

all theses messages growing up, and I adjudicate myself against them. Due to the goals that I have established, I hold myself to these standards and every time something goes wrong in my life, I blame myself extremely for not measuring up. I always work hard. I have been taught that hard work pays off at the end, therefore that's what and all I know. I would begin a project all fired up with enthusiasm, then be visited by negative critics making it difficult to stay positive and focused. The self doubts are in the back of my mind, even if I am a positive person generally. These are thoughts that are waiting to bounce. Without a doubt I have been hard on myself than anyone could ever been on me.

The major challenge of being my worst critic is that it's really a cover up of self sabotage. It took ages to be aware of this. I have heard about the power of positive thinking and how what you think affects what you do. It's hard to remain optimistic when you are posed with pessimistic thoughts. But I learned it's important to be my own best friend. I constantly remind myself that I am deserving of the good things, I am deserving of success. I work extremely hard, I do my best and already successful because I at least had the courage to do something about it, which is more than most, can say. I get rid of those dysfunctional negative believes. I focus on the positive and concentrate on the good-things like tasks that I have achieved, how far I have come overall. To know that I am more knowledgeable today than I was before, so I embrace the wise and developed self now and again, to acknowledge my progress, regardless how minor it maybe. Pessimism only brings disservice every time I engaged in it, it affects my attitude entirely.

I used to put myself down due to my mistakes. I often felt inadequate, stupid, guilty and remorseful. I still get caged in self demolish web occasionally, but I snap myself out of it rapidly and combat not to get stuck in it. It helps to not take things too seriously and to lighten up. How does one take things less seriously though? I think acceptance is the initial step. All too frequent, I justify and defend instead of admitting that it did not work. This happens with majority of people; we need to learn and grow from the past. Be grateful for good things we have in our lives. To recognize that it's a big life, your current situation is only a chapter of your life, maybe even a page. This is not saying we should not learn from where we are, but merely suggesting that we keep a rational and open minded perspective.

In addition to this, I realize that I would not be as hard on others as I am hard on myself, if they had made the same mistakes. Therefore, where is it written that I or you should be above making mistakes?

We do not have to understand all the reasons why things are the way they are. It would be great to get a profound understanding, but I can't always have all the rationale behind everything that occurs. I can spend time trying to understand the root instead of picking up the fruit. You need to just learn what you can and move on.

It's important to forgive ourselves for our shortcomings. I had to learn to develop a thicker skin to protect my soft heart. It helps to have people who believe in you. By being aware, trusting myself and forgiving myself and not taking myself to seriously, I am be able to move from the self demolish mode and build it into being a more esteemed individual.

So every time you do something, do the very best you can and realize that every time you do something it may not be as good as you would have like it to be or as good as it was the first time. That is being human. We need to keep trying and know that your efforts have immense capacity to change your life, whatever it maybe. And keep in mind your efforts will constantly be challenged to test you. We do not always like the challenges life throws at us, but it gives us a platform to learn a great deal about who we are. It's vital to realizes that at the end of day, the person congratulating you the hardest will be yourself. Get to acknowledge yourself for completing each step along the way. That adds up a lot of positive internal reinforcement. The more often something gets well done, the more you build your self esteem as someone successful and that makes you feel great. Instead of rewarding yourself only when you reach the peak of your goal. When self esteem is alive and well, you tend to live from the inside out. You pay attention to the smarts and the strengths; you cut yourself some slack and others too.

LEARNING TO GIVE BACK . . . .

G iving has immense leverage to change the world. It's a tool of power that's beyond us which works with our part in giving back. The principle assures what is given to others, will be given back to you in abundance.

One way or the other, we benefit from society, our families and friends. We need to give back as well. We need to contribute in shaping a better world for all of us through the activity. Although we might not be aware of it, everyone has the ability to make a difference, regardless of how small or big it is. Giving illustrates a selfless character within ourselves that we usually not exposed to. Giving is a human quality that has potential to make the world a better place. There are variety of ways that one can give, it can be through giving time, giving knowledge or love to those in need. Instead of being the one asking for help and waiting to be given, rather think of what can you do to change someone's life to make it a little better? The activity should not feel as a tedious process, it has to begin from a personal will; a character disregarding one's financial and material position. Be the one to meet others needs for a change, this can really go a long way. Adapt gladly to rendering services without expectations and seek to improve self worth and others.

It's important to recognize that you can make a difference within yourself, home, society and eventually the world at large through making a decision to be involved in the growth of others. This just reminds me how we are seized in the mentality of acquiring more and more possessions in our lives we don't necessarily need. This happens to me all time; I purchase clothes to often even when I don't need to. Yes, I agree that clothing is a major weakness for women. But again, it's a waste if you going to be piling up clothes you don't wear and used. Therefore, I learn to give to those who are in need, in that way I contribute to a giving cycle and the next person can also help in a same way. Eventually in our own little helpful acts, we are working towards making a better place for others.

We think we first need to achieve in our lives to be in the position to give back. This is not how it should be, we come into this world with nothing, and we are going to leave the world in same way. The nature of a human being has compelled us to quest for more irrespective of what we have. We consumed in the urge of obtaining in abundance, that we lose sight of what can give substantial fulfillment in our lives.

INVOLVE GOD IN YOUR LIFE

I spent most my life making plans and trying to carry them out. I made long term and short term plans on how my life should turn out and what I am going to do tomorrow, next week, next year or even where I should be in the next five years? I plan on what kind of a job I want, what kind of person I want spend the rest of my life with and what kind of lifestyle I want to live. I plan on the ideal car and house I would like to have.

As I grow up with all the dreams and plans I have as child. I look forward to my future and build hopes and dreams around them. A future I have long waited for, where I will live my dreams and what I have planned all my life. With the dreams that I have, I do what is required to achieve established goals. I live for my dreams and my plans. At this moment, I came to hit the unexpected, that my plans have not materialized as I expected? Why do my dreams fail me? Why plans do not yield as I have foreseen. I spend most of my life living for things that have not occurred or are not really significant for me. What is it that I have been missing? What is it I am not doing, that I should have been doing?

Although I have made plans in my life, God on the other hand has a plan for me that I do not know of. Above all this, whatever I plan, wish and dream for in life. God wants us to live for Him. We need to seek God before anything else. God wants us to serve Him. God wants us to acknowledge Him. God is the architect of our lives. For that mere reason we need to place Him first in everything we do. Once our place with God is right, then other aspects in our lives also falls into place. We need to serve God, as He knows what our needs and wants are. We need to know Him first before anything. He wants us to live a life that is fulfilling and rewarding. He wants us to understand that life is not merely about living for our dreams and plans, but it's about living for Him. God makes plans for us, he works out all the details so that we can live life that pleases and serves Him. God gives and use various facets of our life so we get to understand that our purpose is to glorify Him.

Every time we make plans, the first thing we think of our own selfish reason and motives. We fail to involve God in our plans. The time has arrived to involve God in what you do; you find that plans fail to prosper due to lack of God's presence. His plans are wiser than our plans. Our plans consider only a few short years, but a God's plan considers all the eternality. We need to stubbornly pin our hope on God. He is supremely above your entire gigantic mountain. He has all it takes to dismantle adversities that hinder your progress. Before we can archive anything, we need to lower ourselves to God and apply corrective advice without misgivings.